Clubland

by the same author
and also available from Methuen

Starstruck & The No Boys Cricket Club
The Gift

ROYAL COURT

Royal Court Theatre presents

CLUBLAND

by Roy Williams

First performance at the Royal Court Jerwood Theatre Upstairs,
Sloane Square, London on 15 June 2001.

Supported by Jerwood New Playwrights.

CLUBLAND

by **Roy Williams**

Cast in order of appearance
Ben **Marc Warren**
Kenny **Rhashan Stone**
Ade **Deobia Oparei**
Sandra **Natasha Gordon**
Nathan **Cavan Clerkin**

Director **Indhu Rubasingham**
Designer **Simon Higlett**
Lighting Designer **Mark Jonathan**
Sound Designer **Paul Arditti**
Assistant Director **Emma Wolukau-Wanambwa**
Casting **Lisa Makin, Amy Ball**
Production Manager **Sue Bird**
Company Stage Manager **Cath Binks**
Stage Management **Sharon Cooper, Emily Danby**
Costume Supervisor **Suzanne Duffy**
Company Voice Work **Patsy Rodenburg**

Royal Court Theatre would like to thank the following for their help with this production:
Chelsea Audio Visual Centre, Paul Allen, www.knutz.com, Equinox Nightclub, Ann Summers, Virgin
Megastore, Pocket Phone Shop, Wardrobe care by Persil and Comfort courtesy of Lever Brothers Ltd.

JERWOOD
NEW PLAYWRIGHTS

Since 1993 Jerwood New Playwrights have contributed to some of the Royal Court's most successful productions, including SHOPPING AND FUCKING by Mark Ravenhill (co-production with Out of Joint), EAST IS EAST by Ayub Khan-Din (co-production with Tamasha), THE BEAUTY QUEEN OF LEENANE by Martin McDonagh (co-production with Druid Theatre Company), THE WEIR by Conor McPherson, REAL CLASSY AFFAIR by Nick Grosso, THE FORCE OF CHANGE by Gary Mitchell, ON RAFTERY'S HILL by Marina Carr (co-production with Druid Theatre Company), 4.48 PSYCHOSIS by Sarah Kane and UNDER THE BLUE SKY by David Eldridge.

The Jerwood Charitable Foundation is a registered charity dedicated to imaginative and responsible funding and sponsorship of the arts, education, design and other areas of human endeavour and excellence. This season Jerwood New Playwrights are supporting PRESENCE by David Harrower, HERONS by Simon Stephens and CLUBLAND by Roy Williams.

www.jerwood.org.uk

UNDER THE BLUE SKY by David Eldridge
(photo: Ivan Kyncl)

EAST IS EAST by Ayub Khan-Din
(photo: Robert Day)

THE COMPANY

Roy Williams (writer)
For the Royal Court: Lift Off.
Theatre includes: The Gift (Birmingham Rep); Local Boy (Hampstead); Night and Day (Theatre Venture); The No-Boys Cricket Club (Theatre Royal Stratford East); Josie's Boys (Red Ladder); Starstruck (Tricycle); Souls (Theatre Centre).
Radio includes: Homeboys, Tell Tale (BBC)
Roy received a Writer's Guild nomination for Best New Writer Award in 1996 and a TAPS nomination for Writer of the Year 1996 for The No-Boys Cricket Club. He was the first recipient of the Alfred Fagon Award and the winner of the John Whiting Award 1997 for Starstruck. Roy was joint winner of the George Devine Award 2000 for Lift Off.

Paul Arditti (sound designer)
Paul Arditti has been designing sound for theatre since 1983. He currently combines his post as Head of Sound at the Royal Court (where he has designed more than 60 productions) with regular freelance projects.
Royal Court productions include: Blasted, Mouth To Mouth, Spinning Into Butter, I Just Stopped By To See The Man, Far Away, My Zinc Bed, 4.48 Psychosis, Fireface, Mr Kolpert, The Force of Change, Hard Fruit, Other People, Dublin Carol, The Glory of Living, The Kitchen, Rat in the Skull, Some Voices, Mojo, The Weir, The Steward of Christendom, Shopping and Fucking, Blue Heart (co-productions with Out of Joint); The Chairs (co-production with Theatre de Complicite); Cleansed, Via Dolorosa.
Other theatre includes: Tales From Hollywood (Donmar); Light (Complicite); Our Lady of Sligo (RNT with Out of Joint); Some Explicit Polaroids (Out of Joint); Hamlet, The Tempest (RSC); Orpheus Descending, Cyrano de Bergerac, St Joan (West End); Marathon (Gate).
Musicals includes: Doctor Dolittle, Piaf, The Threepenny Opera.
Awards include: Drama Desk Award for Outstanding Sound Design 1992 for Four Baboons Adoring the Sun (Broadway).

Cavan Clerkin
Theatre includes: Bohemian Lights (Teatro Technics); Stars in the Morning Sky (Camden Peoples' Theatre); Bloody Poetry (White Bear); Night School (Link Theatre); The Rehearsal (Actors Centre).
Television includes: Los Dos Bros, Jonathan Creek, The Strangerers, Smack the Pony, People Like Us, Fatal Embrace, Things to Do in Hoxton When You're Dead, The Lying Game.
Film includes: Carbon Miranda, It Was an Accident, Gangster No 1, The Mild Bunch, Young Americans, Enter the Dragon From Behind, Shiner: A Tale from the Village.

Natasha Gordon
Theatre includes: Top Girls (BAC); Arabian Nights (Young Vic/international/national tour).
Television includes: The Bill.

Simon Higlett (designer)
For the Royal Court: The Force of Change.
Theatre includes: A Russian in the Woods, Medea (RSC); Playboy of the Western World (Liverpool Playhouse); Long Day's Journey into Night, The Accused, The Chiltern Hundreds, A Song at Twilight (West End); Naked Justice (West Yorkshire Playhouse); Beyond a Joke (tour); The Country Wife (Shakespeare Theatre Washington DC); Mrs Warren's Profession, Peer Gynt, The Brothers Karamazov (Manchester Royal Exchange); The Barchester Chronicles, Our Betters, Beethoven's Tenth, Mansfield Park, The Miser, A Doll's House, Rope, Dangerous Corner, Three Sisters, Scenes from a Marriage (Chichester); The Prisoner of Second Avenue, Antony and Cleopatra, The Taming of the Shrew, Lady Windermere's Fan (Haymarket); Talking Heads (Comedy); Kean (Old Vic); The Magistrate (Savoy); In a Little World of our Own (Donmar); The Ride Down Mount Morgan (Derby).
Opera includes: Resurrection (Houston Grand Opera); The Barber of Seville (Germany); Don Giovanni, La Traviata, La Cenerentola, The Marriage of Figaro, The Magic Flute (Music Theatre London).
Simon was Head of Design at the New Shakespeare Company 1986-9.

Mark Jonathan (lighting designer)
For the Royal Court: In the Blood, Class Enemy.
Other recent theatre includes: Honk!, The Waiting Room, Titus Andronicus, Skylight (RNT); Marlene (West End/Paris/Broadway); Sweet Charity (Victoria Palace); The Ha'penny Bridge (Cork Opera House); Jumpers (Birmingham Rep); God & Stephen Hawking (Bath Theatre Royal); Snake in the Grass (Old Vic).
Opera: most recently Peter Grimes, Don Pasquale (Los Angeles Opera) and many productions in Britain, Belgium, France, Germany, Italy, Ireland, Israel, and USA.
Dance includes: The Seasons, Giselle, The Protecting Veil, Far From the Madding Crowd, Powder, The Prospect Before Us, The Two Pigeons, Dante Sonata, Enigma Variations (Birmingham Royal Ballet); Landschaft und Errinerung, Exilium (Stuttgart Ballet).
Mark's designs were selected to represent Great Britain in the 1999 Prague Quadrennial. He has been head of lighting at the Royal National Theatre since 1993.

Deobia Oparei

Theatre includes: Troilus & Cressida, The White Devil, Haroun & The Sea of Stories (RNT); Six Degrees of Separation, Angels in America (Sydney Theatre Company); The Winter's Tale (Theatre de Complicite); Death and the King's Horsemen (Royal Exchange); Cymbeline, Faustus, A Clockwork Orange, A Midsummer Night's Dream (RSC); The Broken Heart, Drums in the Night, The Bells (Leicester Haymarket); Woza Albert (Terra Nova Productions); Romeo and Juliet (Albany Empire).

Film includes: The Four Feathers, South West Nine, Moulin Rouge, Doom Runners, Dark City, Aliens III.

Television includes: Metrosexuality, Smile, Trial and Retribution, Wildside, Gallow Glass, Between the Lines, The Good Guys, Minder, Desmonds, Bloodrights, The Wild Side.

Radio includes: The Gods are Not to Blame, Death Catches the Hunter.

Indhu Rubasingham (director)

For the Royal Court: Lift Off, The Crutch (Young Writers' Festival 1998), The Separation, Business as Unusual (Young Writers' Festival 1996). Other theatre includes: Ramayana (Olivier, RNT/Birmingham Rep); The Waiting Room (Cottosloe, RNT); Time of Fire, Kahini (Birmingham Rep); D'yer Eat with your Fingers!?, D'yer Eat with your Fingers - the Remix, No Boys' Cricket Club, Gulp Fiction (Theatre Royal Stratford East); Sugar Dollies, Shakuntala (Gate); Starstruck (Tricycle); A Doll's House (Young Vic Studio) Voices on the Wind (RNT Studio); River Sutra (Three Mill Island, co-production with the RNT Studio).

Indhu was an Associate Director of the Gate (recipient of Karabe Award 96-97) and recently Associate Director at Birmingham Rep.

Indhu's next production will be The Secret Rapture at Chichester.

Rhashan Stone

Theatre includes: Henry VI, Richard III, Hamlet, Much Ado About Nothing, Camino Real (RSC); Present Laughter, The Tempest, The Seagull (West Yorkshire Playhouse); Sweeney Todd, The Red Balloon (RNT); The Merry Wives Of Windsor, A Funny Thing Happened On the Way to the Forum (New Shakespeare Company); Animal Crackers (Royal Exchange); As You Like It (Cheek by Jowl, world tour); Happy End (Nottingham Playhouse); Chasing the Moment (RNT Studio, BAC, Pleasance); Generations of the Dead in the Abyss of Coney Island Madness (Contact); Five Guys Named Moe (Lyric).

Television includes: Picking up the Pieces, The Detectives, Goodnight Sweetheart, Desmonds, The Blind Date (film short).

Marc Warren

Theatre includes: Privates on Parade, East, Teechers, Salt of the Earth, Plough and the Stars (Haymarket, Leicester); To Kill a Mocking Bird (York Theatre Royal); Kingdom of Earth (Redgrave, Farnham); Out of the Sun (Nuffield, Southampton); Volpone (Almeida); Summer Breeze (Gate); Kes (Snap Theatre Company, UK tour).

Television includes: Oliver Twist, Vice I & II, Bombmaker, Men Only, Band of Brothers, Black Cab, Pretending to be Judith, Oliver Twist, How Do You Want Me?, Wycliffe Christmas Special, Highlander, Fight for Thirteen, Ghostbusters of East Finchley, Touch of Frost, Prime Suspect, The Young Indiana Jones Chronicles, A Martial Kind of Man, Sharpe's Company, The Bill, Heartbeat, Between the Lines, An Ungentlemanly Act, Sam Saturday, Casualty, Gawain and the Green Knight.

Film includes: Shine, Boston Kickout, Al's Lads, Alice Through the Looking Glass, Suburban Psycho, The Real Thing, Dad Savage, Bring Me the Head of Mavis Davis, B Monkey, Dance with the Devil.

Emma Wolukau-Wanambwa

(assistant director)

Emma was most recently an assistant director at the RSC.

As director theatre includes: Object, Tricky, Try Not to Worry (Tart Gallery); Heartpiece (The Other Place); Ghost From a Perfect Place (Chats Palace).

THE ENGLISH STAGE COMPANY AT THE ROYAL COURT

The English Stage Company at the Royal Court opened in 1956 as a subsidised theatre producing new British plays, international plays and some classical revivals.

The first artistic director George Devine aimed to create a writers' theatre, 'a place where the dramatist is acknowledged as the fundamental creative force in the theatre and where the play is more important than the actors, the director, the designer'. The urgent need was to find a contemporary style in which the play, the acting, direction and design are all combined. He believed that 'the battle will be a long one to continue to create the right conditions for writers to work in'.

Devine aimed to discover 'hard-hitting, uncompromising writers whose plays are stimulating, provocative and exciting'. The Royal Court production of John Osborne's Look Back in Anger in May 1956 is now seen as the decisive starting point of modern British drama and the policy created a new generation of British playwrights. The first wave included John Osborne, Arnold Wesker, John Arden, Ann Jellicoe, N F Simpson and Edward Bond. Early seasons included new international plays by Bertolt Brecht, Eugène Ionesco, Samuel Beckett, Jean-Paul Sartre and Marguerite Duras.

The theatre started with the 400-seat proscenium arch Theatre Downstairs, and then in 1969 opened a second theatre, the 60-seat studio Theatre Upstairs. Some productions transfer to the West End, such as Caryl Churchill's Far Away, Conor McPherson's The Weir, Kevin Elyot's Mouth to Mouth and My Night With Reg. The Royal Court also co-produces plays which have transferred to the West End or toured internationally, such as Sebastian Barry's The Steward of Christendom and Mark Ravenhill's Shopping and Fucking (with Out of Joint), Martin McDonagh's The Beauty Queen Of Leenane (with Druid Theatre Company), Ayub Khan-Din's East is East (with Tamasha Theatre Company, and now a feature film).

Since 1994 the Royal Court's artistic policy has again been vigorously directed to finding and producing a new generation of playwrights. The writers include Joe Penhall, Rebecca Prichard, Michael Wynne, Nick Grosso, Judy Upton, Meredith Oakes, Sarah Kane, Anthony Neilson, Judith Johnson, James Stock, Jez Butterworth, Marina Carr, Simon Block, Martin McDonagh, Mark Ravenhill, Ayub Khan-Din, Tamantha Hammerschlag, Jess Walters, Che Walker, Conor McPherson, Simon Stephens, Richard Bean, Roy Williams, Gary Mitchell, Mick Mahoney, Rebecca

photo: Andy Chopping

Gilman, Christopher Shinn, Kia Corthron, David Gieselmann, Marius von Mayenburg and David Eldridge. This expanded programme of new plays has been made possible through the support of A.S.K Theater Projects, the Jerwood Charitable Foundation, the American Friends of the Royal Court Theatre and many in association with the Royal National Theatre Studio.

In recent years there have been record-breaking productions at the box office, with capacity houses for Jez Butterworth's Mojo, Sebastian Barry's The Steward of Christendom, Martin McDonagh's The Beauty Queen of Leenane, Ayub Khan-Din's East is East, Eugène Ionesco's The Chairs, David Hare's My Zinc Bed and Conor McPherson's The Weir, which transferred to the West End in October 1998 and ran for nearly two years at the Duke of York's Theatre.

The newly refurbished theatre in Sloane Square opened in February 2000, with a policy still inspired by the first artistic director George Devine. The Royal Court is an international theatre for new plays and new playwrights, and the work shapes contemporary drama in Britain and overseas.

REBUILDING THE ROYAL COURT

In 1995, the Royal Court was awarded a National Lottery grant through the Arts Council of England, to pay for three quarters of a £26m project to completely rebuild our 100-year old home. The rules of the award required the Royal Court to raise £7.6m in partnership funding. The building has been completed thanks to the generous support of those listed below.

We are particularly grateful for the contributions of over 5,700 audience members.

Royal Court Registered Charity number 231242.

THE AMERICAN FRIENDS OF THE ROYAL COURT THEATRE

AFRCT support the mission of the Royal Court and are primarily focused on raising funds to enable the theatre to produce new work by emerging American writers. Since this not-for-profit organisation was founded in 1997, AFRCT has contributed to seven productions including Rebecca Gilman's Spinning Into Butter. They have also supported the participation of young artists in the Royal Court's acclaimed International Residency.

If you would like to support the ongoing work of the Royal Court, please contact the Development Department on 020 7565 5050.

THE ARTS COUNCIL OF ENGLAND

PROGRAMME SUPPORTERS

The Royal Court (English Stage Company Ltd) receives its principal funding from London Arts. It is also supported financially by a wide range of private companies and public bodies and earns the remainder of its income from the box office and its own trading activities.

The Royal Borough of Kensington & Chelsea gives an annual grant to the Royal Court Young Writers' Programme and the London Boroughs Grants Committee provides project funding for a number of play development initiatives.

The Jerwood Charitable Foundation continues to support new plays by new playwrights through the Jerwood New Playwrights series. Since 1993 the A.S.K. Theater Projects of Los Angeles has funded a Playwrights' Programme at the theatre. Bloomberg Mondays, the Royal Court's reduced price ticket scheme, is supported by Bloomberg.

Sky has also generously committed to a two-year sponsorship of the Royal Court Young Writers' Festival.

AWARDS FOR
THE ROYAL COURT

Terry Johnson's Hysteria won the 1994 Olivier Award for Best Comedy, and also the Writers' Guild Award for Best West End Play. Kevin Elyot's My Night with Reg won the 1994 Writers' Guild Award for Best Fringe Play, the Evening Standard Award for Best Comedy, and the 1994 Olivier Award for Best Comedy. Joe Penhall was joint winner of the 1994 John Whiting Award for Some Voices. Sebastian Barry won the 1995 Writers' Guild Award for Best Fringe Play, the 1995 Critics' Circle Award and the 1997 Christopher Ewart-Biggs Literary Prize for The Steward of Christendom, and the 1995 Lloyds Private Banking Playwright of the Year Award. Jez Butterworth won the 1995 George Devine Award for Most Promising Playwright, the 1995 Writers' Guild New Writer of the Year Award, the Evening Standard Award for Most Promising Playwright and the 1995 Olivier Award for Best Comedy for Mojo.

The Royal Court won the 1995 Prudential Award for Theatre and was the overall winner of the 1995 Prudential Award for the Arts for creativity, excellence, innovation and accessibility. The Royal Court Theatre Upstairs won the 1995 Peter Brook Empty Space Award for innovation and excellence in theatre.

Michael Wynne won the 1996 Meyer-Whitworth Award for The Knocky. Martin McDonagh won the 1996 George Devine Award, the 1996 Writers' Guild Best Fringe Play Award, the 1996 Critics' Circle Award and the 1996 Evening Standard Award for Most Promising Playwright for The Beauty Queen of Leenane. Marina Carr won the 19th Susan Smith Blackburn Prize (1996/7) for Portia Coughlan. Conor McPherson won the 1997 George Devine Award, the 1997 Critics' Circle Award and the 1997 Evening Standard Award for Most Promising Playwright for The Weir. Ayub Khan-Din won the 1997 Writers' Guild Award for Best West End Play, the 1997 Writers' Guild New Writer of the Year Award and the 1996 John Whiting Award for East is East. Anthony Neilson won the 1997 Writers' Guild Award for Best Fringe Play for The Censor.

At the 1998 Tony Awards, Martin McDonagh's The Beauty Queen of Leenane (co-production with Druid Theatre Company) won four awards including Garry Hynes for Best Director and was nominated for a further two. Eugene Ionesco's The Chairs (co-production with Theatre de Complicite) was nominated for six Tony awards. David Hare won the 1998 Time Out Live Award for Outstanding Achievement and six awards in New York including the Drama League, Drama Desk and New York Critics Circle Award for Via Dolorosa. Sarah Kane won the 1998 Arts Foundation Fellowship in Playwriting. Rebecca Prichard won the 1998 Critics' Circle Award for Most Promising Playwright for Yard Gal (co-production with Clean Break).

Conor McPherson won the 1999 Olivier Award for Best New Play for The Weir. The Royal Court won the 1999 ITI Award for Excellence in International Theatre. Sarah Kane's Cleansed was judged Best Foreign Language Play in 1999 by Theater Heute in Germany. Gary Mitchell won the 1999 Pearson Best Play Award for Trust. Rebecca Gilman was joint winner of the 1999 George Devine Award and won the 1999 Evening Standard Award for Most Promising Playwright for The Glory of Living.

Roy Williams and Gary Mitchell were joint winners of the George Devine Award 2000 for Most Promising Playwright for Lift Off and The Force of Change respectively. At the Barclays Theatre Awards 2000 presented by the TMA, Richard Wilson won the Best Director Award for David Gieselmann's Mr Kolpert and Jeremy Herbert won the Best Designer Award for Sarah Kane's 4.48 Psychosis. Gary Mitchell won the Evening Standard's Charles Wintour Award 2000 for Most Promising Playwright for The Force of Change. Stephen Jeffreys' I Just Stopped by to See The Man won an AT&T: On Stage Award 2000. David Eldridge's Under the Blue Sky won the Time Out Live Award 2001 for Best New Play in the West End.

In 1999, the Royal Court won the European theatre prize New Theatrical Realities, presented at Taormina Arte in Sicily, for its efforts in recent years in discovering and producing the work of young British dramatists.

ROYAL COURT BOOKSHOP

The bookshop offers a wide range of playtexts, theatre books, screenplays and art-house videos with over 1,000 titles. Located in the downstairs Bar and Food area, the bookshop is open Monday to Saturday, afternoons and evenings.

Many Royal Court playtexts are available for just £2 including the plays in the current season and recent works by David Hare, Conor McPherson, Martin Crimp, Sarah Kane, David Mamet, Gary Mitchell, Martin McDonagh, Ayub Khan-Din, Jim Cartwright and Rebecca Prichard. We offer a 10% reduction to students on a range of titles.
Further information : 020 7565 5024

FOR THE ROYAL COURT

Clubland

Roy Williams

Methuen Drama

Published by Methuen 2001

1 3 5 7 9 10 8 6 4 2

First published in Great Britain in 2001 by
Methuen Publishing Limited
215 Vauxhall Bridge Road, London SW1V 1EJ

Methuen Publishing Limited Reg. No. 3543167

A CIP catalogue record for this book is available from the British Library

ISBN 0 413 76950 X

Typeset by SX Composing DTP, Rayleigh, Essex
Printed and bound in Great Britain by
Cox & Wyman Ltd, Reading, Berkshire

Act One

Scene One

Palais nightclub (Eighties night).

Kenny *and* **Ben** *come out of the gents loo. They stand and drool by the fruit machine as they watch girls coming out of the ladies. Music is heard in the background. They both start singing along, making up their own lyric to the song that is being played over. They are both drunk.*

Ben . . . get down on it . . .

Kenny . . . suck my helmet . . .

Ben . . . please don't bite it . . .

Together . . . juss excite it! (*Louder.*) . . . get down on it, suck my helmet, please don't bite it, juss excite it!

Boys laugh. Another pop song plays.

Ben I don't know the lines to this one. Tell the guy to play Adam and the Ants or summin.

Kenny Yu tell him. Eighties night is gettin shit.

Ben Pussy round the clock!

Kenny They ain't all that.

Ben Get on the floor and do sum moves. (*Pushes him.*)

Kenny I ain't dancin to this. There ain't no one on the floor. Except that African and dem girls over there. Look at the prat.

Ben He's getting amongst it.

Kenny He's so black he's blue.

Ben He's getting started.

Kenny Right sooty.

Ben   Kenny, will yu please get yer arse on the dance floor and show them how it's done.

Kenny   I got all night.

Ben   They're gonna get taken if yu don't move now.

Kenny   Yu go. Yu wanted to come here, I wanted to go up West.

Ben   We always come here.

Kenny   Look how's he's going for them.

Ben   I know.

Kenny   Could he be any more obvious?

Ben   He's having fun.

Kenny   He calls that dancing?

Ben   I don't see them complaining.

Kenny   How old yu reckon?

Ben   Ate een.

Kenny   Wat dog years? (*Presses collect button.*)

Ben   Why yu do that?

Kenny   Saving yer money.

Ben   Yer name Denise? (**Kenny** *taps him on the cheek.*) Get off.

Kenny   Rang Nathan the other day.

Ben   So?

Kenny   Left a message. Melanie musta had the baby by now.

Ben (*so not interested*)   Triffic.

Kenny (*points at sooty*)   Yu really reckon I'm a better dancer than him?

Ben   Look, juss go up and dance near them, show dem yer moves, catch their eyes and that. Go on.

Kenny   Patience, boy, I know wat I'm doin. Yu juss go play wid yer cherries. (*Sees something.*) Oh my God! (*Nudges* **Ben**.)

Ben   Wat!

Kenny *points to* **Ade** (*sooty*) *who enters. The boys continue to stare at him as he approaches the loo door.* **Kenny** *whispers something to* **Ben**.

Ade   Yeah?

Ben   Ade Boateng, ennit.

Ade   Do I know yu?

Ben   Manor House School.

Ade   Name would help.

Ben   Ben Harper.

Ade   Stevie's brother!

Ben   Yeah, man.

Ade   Awright, man, how's tricks?

Ben   Awright.

Ade   Who's yer friend?

Kenny   Kenny Taylor. Remember me?

Ade   Vaguely.

Ben   Doing awright?

Ade   This and that.

Ben   Yeah, I can see this and that from here.

Ade   Come early yu get the best ones, ennit.

Ben   Damn, man, how yu get so big?

Ade   Few hours down the gym, press-ups. Thirty a day, every day.

Ben   Thass a how yu get the six pack?

Ade   Come wid me, get yu off dem kebabs.

Ben (*prods* **Ade**'s *chest*)   No fat, not an inch. Kenny yu gotta touch this come.

Kenny   Get off. (**Ben** *drops to the floor.*) Wat yu doin?

Ben   Like this, Ade?

Ade   Spread yer legs a bit. Now push. Harder.

Kenny   Get up.

The best **Ben** *can manage is four press-ups. He sits up, sweating.*

Ade   Is that the best yu can do?

Ben   I'm fucked.

Ade   I know a guy once, couldn't do more than five press-ups without sweating, had a heart attack when he was thirty, kill him.

Ben   Yu joke?

Ben *puts his beer away. He tries to take* **Kenny**'s *bottle off him.*

Kenny   Get off me.

Ben   Yu wanna die before yer thirty?

Kenny   Yu wanna act like a sheep gwan, move yerself.

Ade   I see yer later, girls.

Ben   Ade, hold up, man. Don't suppose yu could see yer way thru lettin us in on sum of the action, yu nuh. I mean yu ain't gonna have all three a' dem.

Ade   I could if I wanted to. Tell yu wat, gimme a minute, then come over.

Kenny   Wat about Denise?

Ade Who?

Kenny He's married.

Ben Love to open yer mout, ennit.

Kenny Kiss my arse.

Ben Suck my dick.

Ade Guys! Wass 'appenin?

Ben We're coming.

Ade One second yeah. (*Exits.*)

Ben Yeah, man! Yu ready?

Kenny Vaguely knows me my arse. Fool only sat next to me in class.

Ben I can't believe thass him.

Kenny Wat is yer name?

Ben He was so skinny.

Kenny Kunta, Kunta Kinte! (*Pretends to crack a whip.*) Yer name is Toby! Kunta Kinte! (*Laughs.*) Remember that?

Ben Say that to his face now. I dare yu.

Kenny Yu think I won't? I ain't kissin his arse like yu. All that press-up shit, wat was all that about?

Ade *comes back out.*

Ade Awright, come. (*Leaves.*)

Ben Come.

Kenny Ware yu goin? Let's juss wait.

Ben I don't wanna wait.

Kenny Yu tellin me yu want hang round wid Ade Boateng?

Ben I wanna enjoy myself.

Kenny   Awright, let's go.

Ben   Don't gimme no grief, man.

Kenny   Shut up.

Ben   No dropping of Denise into the conversation.

Kenny   Yu mean yer wife.

Ben   See thass the shit I'm talking about.

Kenny   I won't.

Ben   Yu might get a bit too, yer nuh. Juss don't do yer pussy act.

Kenny   Is who yu callin pussy?

Scene Two

Sandra's *living room.*

Ade *is trying to watch tele.* **Sandra** *is chatting away on her mobile.*

Sandra   . . . cos he's a fuckin bastard thass why! I mean who the fuck does he think he is? He ain't nuttin! The second I fuckin lay eye on him right, I told the girl I say 'Nicole, Nicole, darlin, that Brendan of yours ain't nuttin, he ain't worth shit, he's a fuckin crackhead, drop him.' But nuh she comes back wid, 'Nuh nuh, Sandra, he ain't like that, yu don't know him like I do!' She find out now though ennit, she fuckin know wid her empty purse, empty bank account, empty flat. He fleeced her good, TV, video, radio, anything that wasn't nailed down, he even fuckin teif her little kid's playstation man, juss so that he can buy his fuckin shit and get fuckin high. Hear how she try tellin me it was a burglary and Brendan had nuttin to do wid it. Carryin on like I got stupid written on my fuckin forehead.

Ade *tries to get into the movie, but gives up, he turns it off with the remote.* **Ade** *looks away clearly disgusted by* **Sandra**'s *language.*

Sandra   He is lucky he didn't do that in front of me, he is fuckin lucky. Cos I woulda killed him, Sonya, on the Bible I fuckin swear to yu, I woulda killed the cunt! Yu know summin, God forgive me yeah, but I hope he teifs from her again, I hope he teifs from her kid, from her mum, from everybody she knows, robs dem fuckin blind, and I hope I'm there when he does it, I walk right in and catch him in the middle of it, it'll be worth it, Sonya, cos then fuckin watch me, I'll juss pick up the first thing that comes into view, I don't care wat it is, telephone, microwave, a fuckin hammer, I'll bury it into the fucker's head! Then I'll stand over the fucker, watch the fucker bleed to death and laugh my fuckin arse off! Oh Sonya, man, yu shouldn't have told me any of this, who the fuck does he think he is! (*Sudden change in mood.*) So anyway, darlin, how yu doin, yu awright? No. No! Oh darlin, thass fuckin brilliant? So when did he ask? And it's now yu tell me? (*Laughs.*) Well, it's about fuckin time, don't yu think? Sonya gettin married, fer fucks sake, wass the world comin to. Whoa, whoa, wat yu mean yu gotta go, this girl makes me laugh, man, yu tell me yer engaged and yu gotta go, sit yer arse down, woman! Yeah yeah, I suppose, yu gotta go then, ennit, go on move then, yu fuckin lightweight. But yu best call me when yu get back, or I'm comin over deh to kick yer sorry black arse, yu get me? We'll have to go out, it's yer birthday soon, ennit? Yeah, yu too, darlin, be good yeah, love yer too. (*Hangs up. Clocks'* **Ade***'s face.*) Yes?

Ade   Did yer mother ever wash yer mouth out with soap?

Sandra   Yeah, but it didn't do any fuckin good. Shouldn't have bin listen.

Ade   Hard not to.

Sandra   Yu should have words wid him.

Ade   I will.

Sandra   Good.

Ade   I'm playin pool wid him later, I'll buy him a card or summin.

Sandra   Not Sonya and Trevor yu fool!

Ade   Who den?

Sandra   Nicole and that fuckin cunt Brendan.

Ade   Do yu have to swear?

Sandra   Yeah, I fuckin do.

Ade   Every time yu do, I feel sick.

Sandra   Well pardon fuckin me.

Ade   Would it kill yer to be a bit more . . .

Sandra   Wat?

Ade   Sensitive.

Sandra   Yer chat is dry.

Ade   I tell yer, man . . .

Sandra   Are yu gonna have words wid him?

Ade   Why?

Sandra   He's outta order.

Ade   How yu know she ain't on crack herself?

Sandra   Say that again?

Ade   Nicole ain't no Pollyanna right.

Sandra   Go screw.

Ade   Juss let 'em get on wid it. One week from now, they'll be huggin and kissin again.

Sandra   Not if I've got anythin to do wid it.

Ade   Wat yu gonna do?

Sandra   Yu'll find out.

Ade   Yu ain't gonna do shit.

Sandra   Bwoy, move.

Ade   Keep yer nose out.

Sandra   Move.

Ade   Will yu stop talkin like that. Yu ain't Nicole. Yer a sarf London girl, Sandra, deal wid it.

Sandra   Yu know a lot about sarf London girls, ennit.

Ade   Sorry?

Sandra   Nuttin.

Ade   Can I watch my film now?

Sandra   Oh wat for?

Ade   Cos it's good.

Sandra   It's shit.

Ade   Wass up, Sandra, too much hard work for yer?

Sandra   I don't know wat was wrong wid *Men in Black*.

Ade   Yu wanna talk about shit.

Sandra   Juss cos I don't go for none of yer foreign crap, who yu tryin to impress this week, Ade?

Ade   Yu see any subtitles on this one?

Sandra   I still don't like it.

Ade   Yu juss can't handle anythin that requires yu to use yer brain. Has to be obvious, no matter how bad.

Sandra   Wat about this one?

Ade   Don't even try.

Sandra   So obvious it's untrue.

Ade   Yer dreamin.

Sandra   It's him, ennit?

Ade Who?

Sandra The cripple guy.

Ade Not necessarily.

Sandra Bet it is.

Ade How can yu possibly know that?

Sandra He's makin the story up. He's tellin that copper wat he wants to hear.

Ade Yu seen this film, ain't yer?

Sandra No.

Ade Don't lie.

Sandra I ain't lying.

Ade Yu've bloody seen it.

Sandra I ain't.

Ade I really wanted to see this yu know.

Sandra So watch it.

Ade How can I when yu juss told me.

Sandra I might be wrong.

Ade Yu've seen it, Sandra, I know yu have.

Sandra I ain't!

Ade Any time I want to relax.

Sandra I ain't seen it! (*He ignores her.*) Wass the matter wid yer, didn't score lass night?

Ade Wat?

Sandra Yu heard me.

Ade No.

Sandra Yu try to?

Ade   No.

Sandra   Yu go up West?

Ade   I didn't score. I got a girl.

Sandra   Don't touch me.

Ade   Yu got summin to say?

Sandra   Ware were yu all night?

Ade   Oh man, do we have to go through this again?

Sandra   Juss answer the question.

Ade   I told yu, playin cards wid Leroy.

Sandra   Yu didn't phone.

Ade   Yu my mum?

Sandra   I was worried.

Ade   I went straight to work, wass yer problem?

Sandra   Watch the film.

Ade   Wat Sandra?

Sandra   I haven't seen it, I swear to yer.

Ade   Wat!

Sandra   Watch the film!

Ade *goes back to watching the movie. He tries to relax back into it but cannot, he notices* **Sandra** *is staring at him.*

Ade   Fucks sake, wat!

Sandra *slowly unbuttons her shirt to reveal her bra.*

Ade (*getting aroused*)   Yeah, now wat?

Sandra   Get the handcuffs. (**Ade** *laughs.*) Ade, don't make me beg.

Ade   Yu said no last time.

Sandra   Girl can't change her mind?

Ade   Yu do on a regular basis.

Sandra   Juss get them.

Ade *jumps up like a little boy about to open his presents. He exits for a brief moment out of the room.* **Sandra** *feels a little cold, nervous even.* **Ade** *returns with a set of handcuffs.* **Sandra** *surrenders her hands without looking at him.* **Ade** *handcuffs her.*

Ade   Don't look so worried.

Ade *gives her a genuine loving kiss. This calms* **Sandra** *a little. Perhaps it will not be so bad she thinks.* **Ade** *positions himself, he unbuckles his belt, ready to take* **Sandra** *from behind.*

Ade   How deep yu want it?

Sandra   Deep.

Ade   Really deep?

Sandra   Yeah, yeah, really deep . . . (*Bursts out laughing.*) Sorry, sorry!

Ade   You don't want to do it, fuckin say so.

Sandra   Language.

Ade   So why tell me to get the handcuffs?

Sandra   I dunno. Maybe cos I'm tryin to understand yu.

Ade   Understand wat?

Sandra   It's wat yu do wid dem, ennit?

Ade   Whose dem?

Sandra   Will yu please get me out of this.

Ade   No.

Sandra   Ade!

Ade   Yu wanted them, yu stay where yu are.

Sandra   They're hurtin my wrists.

Ade   I'm not a mind-reader, Sandra, wat do yu want from me?

Sandra   Yu not fuckin other girls would be nice.

Ade   I'm not.

Sandra   Don't lie to me.

Ade   Sandra . . .

Sandra   Yvonne saw yu.

Ade   Why yu always believe every word that comes out of her mouth?

Sandra   She saw yu comin outta the Palais wid sum silly little white bitch. The fuckin Palais, Ade. Scraping the bottom of the barrel now, don't yu think?

Ade   How she know it was me?

Sandra   Yu muss tink I'm a right arsehole to mek yer lie so obvious.

Ade   Awright, I went to the Palais, I was chattin to sum white bit on the way out one night, is that a crime?

Sandra   Yu weren't juss chattin, Ade.

Ade   She's lyin about that.

Sandra   Lyin about wat?

Ade   Lyin about watever it is she saw me do.

Sandra   Yu fuckin bastard.

Ade   Oh thass it, ennit? One word from Yvonne the mouth, and I'm tried and convicted.

Sandra   Why would she lie?

Ade   Cos she's a dried-up bitch.

Sandra   She's my mate.

Ade   She ain't no mate, it she yu should be watchin, not me, her.

Sandra   Wat yu chattin about?

Ade   Ask her about New Year's Eve.

Sandra   I'm askin yu.

Ade   Yer brother's party. She had me cornered on the stairs, arms all over me, beggin me to take me upstairs. Horny as fuck. Going on about it's bin years since she free it up for a man, but she'll gladly free it up for me, juss me, and only me. I pushed her away, tell her I didn't want to know, she call me black this . . .

Sandra   Bullshit.

Ade   Black that.

Sandra   Yer lying.

Ade   Thass yer friend.

Sandra   Yu juss love to think every gal in sight wants yu.

Ade   It's the truth.

Sandra   Like any sista's gonna demean herself like that for yu.

Ade   Yu are so naive.

Sandra   Yu and yer fuckin white women.

Ade   Least they ain't frigid.

Sandra   Oh so yu callin me frigid now? Yu didn't say nuttin about me bin frigid when we first went out.

Ade   Things change.

Sandra   Yu ain't makin me feel like this.

Ade   Feel wat yu like.

Sandra   Get the fuck outta my flat. Get the fuck outta my flat.

Ade (*grabs his coat and leaves*)   Frigid bitch.

Sandra   Black bastard! Go chase yer white women!

Sandra *tries again to wriggle out of the handcuffs.*

Sandra   Bastard.

Scene Three

Ben's *back garden.*

Late afternoon.

Ben *is on the ground doing press-ups. He tries to do move than four but gives up. He is panting and sweating as he sits back up.* **Ben** *sits in his deckchair, takes in the sun, and drinks his beer. He reaches for his little tin box on the ground, places it on his lap and starts rolling up a spliff. Sound of a dog barking coming from inside.* **Kenny** *comes running out, he shuts the door quickly behind him.*

Ben   Yu took yer time. Yu better have opened the windows in the toilet, man. Yu awright? Ware's yer beer?

Kenny   In there.

Ben   Well, go get it.

Kenny   Yu are aware there's a big bastard of a dog, runnin around yer house.

Ben   Adolf. Cute, ain't he?

Kenny   Nuh Ben, that ain't a word I'd use. Yu mighta warned me yu bought a dog.

Ben   Forgot.

Kenny   Bollocks yu forgot. Yu plannin on tellin yu were sorry, after the cunt ripped my arse off? Yu called yer fucking dog Adolf?

Ben   I bin trainin him to attack blacks. Nuff burglaries round here committed by yu lot.

Kenny   Yu racist wanker.

Ben   True though.

Kenny   Least we don't rape no women.

Ben   Yu bloody do that as well.

Kenny   Not as much as yu.

Ben (*shouts*)   Adolf? Here, boy!

Kenny   Fuck off, Ben.

Ben (*laughs*)   Look at yer, shittin yerself.

Kenny   Adolf? Watcha yer call him that for?

Ben   Good Aryan name!

Kenny   I bet yu've got swastikas and pictures of Hitler hangin on yer wall when I'm not here. (**Ben** *laughs*.) Don't yer?

Ben   We got 'em put up in the spare room.

Kenny   Gimme the spliff.

Ben   Hold up, there's an art to this.

Kenny   Fuck the art, pass it over.

Ben *finishes rolling it up, he lights up, takes a few puffs before handing it over to* **Kenny***. The lads relax for a minute, enjoying their spliff, drinking their beer. They put on their sunglasses. Dog starts barking.*

Ben   Shut up, yu ain't comin out.

Kenny   Cheers.

Ben   Ain't doin it for yu, they've got a German shepherd next door, he's bin havin it off wid. Horny little bastard. Only got it pregnant. Dogs' owner went all menstral on me, we gotta take summa the pups, our responsibility. (*Dog is howling.*) I didn't even wan' a dog, shut up. Guess who I saw the oder day? That blonde bit from the Palais lass week.

The one whose mate was gettin off wid Ade. She came into the shop, I sold her a pair of trainers.

Kenny   Yer point?

Ben   She was wid her mum. She was shopping for trainers wid her mum. (*Laughing.*)

Kenny   She said she was nineteen.

Ben   Nineteen minus five more like.

Kenny (*disgusted*)   Oh man! Errgh!

Ben   Wat yu crying for, yu didn't do nuttin.

Kenny   Yeah I know but, errgh!

Ben   She was in her school uniform.

Kenny   Errgh!

Ben   It's Ade yu should be worried about. He had his hand right up her mate's skirt, yu see him? She's got sum front though. There she was in the shop, her mum two feet away, standin there in her gymslip, no shame. Coming on to me. Askin about yu. She's up for yer, Kenny, yu coulda had her.

Kenny   Well I'm glad I didn't. Oh man!

Ben   Only reason nuttin happened cos yu were doin yer pussy act.

Kenny   I ain't no pussy right.

Ben   So wat happened?

Kenny   Didn't fancy it. I had a feeling she was a kid.

Ben   Shut up, man, I saw yer, yer tongue was on the floor dread, nuttin happened cos yu were boring the arse off her about yer job. Who gives a fuck about pensions? Yu think she wants to hear that? She was waitin for the jump, man.

Kenny   So wat about yu?

Ben   She weren't my type.

Kenny   Yer full of shit. I prefer women right, not little girls. It's gotta be right. I want it to feel right.

Ben   Don't do a Nathan on me.

Kenny   I'm not doin anything, I'm juss sayin.

Ben   Sayin wat?

Kenny   Don't it make yu tink sumtimes?

Ben   Wat does?

Kenny   Nate. Yu saw the way him and Mel looked at each other.

Ben   Oh man.

Kenny   So how was it for yu when yu first saw Denise then?

Ben   Nice tits. (**Kenny** *shakes his head.*) It was. Awright she made me laugh, we got on, nuttin special. None of this lovey-lovey crap.

Kenny   This is the woman yu married.

Ben   So? Forget Nate. He don't love that girl. He only married it cos he got it pregnant.

Kenny   Shut up.

Ben   It's true.

Kenny   Yu shouldn't say things like that.

Ben   Ask himself if yu don't believe me.

Kenny   I will.

Ben   Do I look as if I care? Now can we stick to the matter in hand please, yu getting a poke.

Kenny   I don't need yer help for that.

Ben   I didn't see yu turnin up yer nose at my help when yu wanted to shag that girl who worked in the shop.

Kenny   Here we go.

Ben   Debbie. Yu borrowed the keys to my car to take her home one night and yu still didn't shag her.

Kenny   She had a boyfriend.

Ben   Funny how she never mentioned no boyfriend to me.

Kenny   She had a boyfriend awright.

Ben   That girl Ade had, she had a boyfriend.

Kenny   How yu know?

Ben   Heard her tell him.

Kenny   So wat?

Ben   Didn't stop Ade though.

Kenny   Don't compare me to him.

Ben   Ooooh!

Kenny   I gotta better taste.

Ben   Yu say so.

Kenny   I do.

Ben   Yu de man.

Kenny   Ennit.

Ben   How long ago was that wid Debbie?

Kenny   Leave it, Ben.

Ben   A year. And how long since yu had it last?

Kenny   Yer askin fer a slap.

Ben   Yer sack mus be bursting. Overflowing, tidal wave!

Kenny   Will yu shut up.

Ben   I gotta get yu layed. I don't care if it's the biggest slag there is.

Kenny   I ain't goin out tonight. And wat about yu, wouldn't Denise like to see a bit more of her husband?

Ben   Denise can kiss my arse.

Kenny   Wass happened now?

Ben   Take yer pick. The way she eats, the way she talks, sleeps, walks. And her teeth, her teeth Kenny.

Kenny   Ain't that noticeable.

Ben   Yer such a liar. She looks like a horse. Yu know wat, I woke up this morning right, I saw her, reading one of her books, mouth wide open wid her bloody teeth, all for the world to see. I was yawning, stretching out my arms an that, I was so tempted to whack her in the side of her mouth wid my elbow, make out it was an accident, didn't see her there, mash up her teeth though, hopefully. I'll be doing her a favour, yu think she's happy looking like that?

Kenny   Yu need help.

Ben   Like I was really gonna do it.

Kenny   Why don't yu juss leave, man?

Ben   And my job too? Her dad's juss made me manager. Four years of shit I took from him to get that.

Kenny   Yu don't love her.

Ben   I married her.

Kenny   Yer point?

Ben   Yer borin me, Kenny.

Kenny   I warned yu not to do it. Like a fool, yu nuh listen to me.

Ben   Rah, hear him chat like a bro now.

Kenny   Fuck off wid that.

Ben   Joke, man!

Kenny   Tryin to help yu.

Ben   So don't help, problem solved. I do wat I please when I please yu get me? So wat time yu comin round tonight?

Kenny   I'm stayin in.

Ben   Oh fer fuck's sake.

Kenny   I'm stayin in.

Ben   Yeah, laters Nathan.

Kenny   Shut it. (*Pauses before opening the door, sound of dog growling.*) Ben?

Ben   Thass my name.

Kenny   I wanna get out.

Ben   I ain't stoppin yer.

Kenny   The dog.

Ben   He don' bite, much.

Kenny   I wanna go home, yer cunt. Awright! I'll come out.

Ben   Nice one.

Kenny   Yu such a kid.

Ben (*goes inside*)   Prince, upstairs, Prince, upstairs. (*Calls.*) Yu can come in now.

Kenny   Prince?

Ben   Did yu really think I'd call my dog Adolf ? Kenny, how long yu known me?

Kenny   Yer a dick.

Ben   Yer not lying to me now?

Kenny   No.

Ben   Good, cos I'll send Prince round after yer. Back here at nine.

Kenny   Yes, Masa. (*Exits.*)

Ben   Yer learnin.

Scene Four

Palais nightclub.

Kenny *is standing with* **Ade** *by the fruit machine.* **Ade** *is looking over at some girls, giving them the eye.*

Ade   Yu don't have to be embarrassed.

Kenny   About wat?

Ade   That yu got a hard-on.

Kenny   Excuse me?

Ade   These girls wouldn't be wearing skirts up to their arses if yu couldn't get a hard-on. That is why they are dressed like that, to get yu hard. Check this one, man.

Kenny   I ain't got a hard-on.

Ade   Yu queer?

Kenny   No.

Ade   So wass yer story? Yer in a club, wall to wall wid trim, an yu don't feel nuttin. Yu queer?

Kenny   Awright I've got one.

Ade   Got wat?

Kenny   A hard-on.

Ade (*laughs*)   Go deh.

Kenny   So wat about yu?

Ade   I ain't tellin yu.

Kenny   I juss told yu.

Ade   So?

Kenny   Yu have.

Ade   Maybe.

Kenny   Got the biggest one there is.

Ade   Maybe not.

Kenny   Yer tongue's on the floor.

Ade   Thass my business, I ain't going round tellin people how big my stiffie is. Yer such a fool, Mr Lame. A dog could do better than yu.

Kenny   Mr Lame. Thass wat we used to call yu at school.

Ade   And other things.

Kenny   I knew yu remembered me.

Ade   My first day at school, couldn't speak much English.

Kenny   Yu couldn't speak any English.

Ade   Teacher asked yu to look after me. Yu were my friend. Yu made my life hell.

Kenny   Wat did I do?

Ade   Wat didn't yu do.

Kenny   Yu were holdin me back.

Ade   From all yer white friends.

Kenny   Yu were stupid.

Ade   I was a foreigner. But it's awright Kenny, it's awright. I forgive yu.

Kenny   Why?

Ade   Why not?

Kenny Yu think yer such a hot guy now, cos yer done yer body up? I ain't impressed. Hangin round wid us like yer a mate or summin. Come on, wat yu want? Tell me.

Ade Gonna beat me up if I don't?

Kenny I never touched yu.

Ade Too busy lettin yer white friends do it. But I understand, why Kenny, yu wanted respect, yu didn't want them pickin on yu.

Kenny I looked after myself.

Ade Blatant lie.

Kenny Oh look, juss fuck off, kunta, yeah.

Ade I'm gonna forget yu said that. This time. But yu call me that again and I'm gonna hurt yu bad, yu understand me?

Kenny I ain't afraid of yu.

Ade Kenny, Kenny, wat made us so different, man? Tell me summin, yu think a white man sees us any different?

Kenny We are different.

Ade Wat is it with yu West Indians? Yu bin hangin round wid Ben too long.

Kenny Move.

Ade He's fucked yu up. and yu know why, cos yu were too busy kissin up dem white boys' backsides.

Kenny I've heard this shit before.

Ade Wantin to be like 'em.

Kenny There ain't nuttin wrong wid me.

Ade Why yu think they beat me up? Cos deh were scared of me, of wat I can do.

Kenny Right.

Ade   I bet yu wanna marry a white girl. Breed wid one a'
dem. Thass sad.

Kenny   Wat yu tink I am?

Ade   Kenny, yu juss admitted to me yu got a hard-on. Yer
still lettin Ben Harper lead yu round like a dog. Yu gotta
tink, brudda. Fuck 'em yeah, by all means, but don't breed
wid dem.

Kenny   I do think. I ain't lettin no white guy run tings.

Ade   Oh, so yer runnin tings?

Kenny   Exactly.

Ade   Well I ain't seein much results.

Kenny   I don't care wat yer seein.

Ade   Look at me. Look at me, Kenny. Look at all dem gal.
Beautiful, young, white gal. Ready. Ripe. Choose one,
choose any gal for me and I got twenty quid in my pocket
that says I'll score. Wat yu don't believe? Three white girls
are starin at me right now. Left over yer shoulder, girl in
blue dancin wid sum bloke. On my right redhead standin by
the bar wearing black, chattin wid her mates. Some blonde
bit, sitting down drinkin a Coke, to yer left. See wat I mean?
Still say yer runnin tings? When's the last time yu fucked a
girl, Kenny? Fuck? Pussy?

Kenny   None of yer business.

Ade   Come on, bro to bro.

Kenny   It's none of yer business. I juss have, thass all yu
need to know. (**Ade** *starts sniffing him.*) Get off me.

Ade   Yu sure yu had pussy?

Kenny   Yes.

Ade   I ain't smellin no pussy.

Kenny   I have.

Ade   So when yu lass have it?

Kenny   Couple of months ago.

Ade   Name?

Kenny   Debbie.

Ade   Yu lie bad.

Kenny   I'm not lyin.

Ade   Fuck me, man.

Kenny   Yeah, fuck yu.

Ade   Yu gotta be the only one I know.

Kenny   I'm not lyin.

Ade   Does Ben know?

Kenny   Listen.

Ade   And yu a bro too!

Kenny   I'm tellin yer . . .

Ade   Do yu not feel the tiniest bit of shame?

Kenny   Her name was Debbie.

Ade   How old are yu?

Kenny   I met her in a bar.

Ade   Yer sad fucker.

Kenny   It's the truth awright.

Ade   Go stand over deh.

Ben *comes out of the loo and joins his mates.*

Ben   Yu bag some trim yet, Ade?

Ade   Eyeing one up now.

Ben   Who who! (*Looks.*) Wat, that fat one?

Ade   Na thass Kenny's.

Ben Yer like 'em big, ennit, Kenny? Yu shoulda seen this bird he pulled a couple of years back, Ade, sum real fat bitch. He had his hands all over her flabby legs and flabby arse man. Best he could get. Ennit, Ken, Kenny?

Kenny Get off me.

Ben Awright don't cry.

Kenny Yer the one who's gonna be cryin.

Ben Look how fat her arse is.

Kenny Yu hear wat I said?

Ben Yu could show a film on it.

Kenny Ben?

Ben Yeah, bitch, I'm chattin about yu.

Kenny Did yu hear wat I said, Ben?

Ben She's tellin her man on me.

Ade Yu ain't 'fraid?

Ben Do I look 'fraid?

Kenny Don't talk to me like that again.

Ben (*to the boyfriend*)   And yer a fat cunt as well, deal wid it.

Kenny (*grabs* **Ben**)   I'll buss yu up right. (**Ben** *laughs*.) Don't laugh at me.

Ben Yer are so moany.

Ade (*sees someone approaching*)   Awright, take it easy, man, we don't wan no trouble yeah.

Ben No, let the wanker come, man.

Without warning and out of nowhere, **Kenny** *shoves his mates out of the way and darts over to the dance floor.*

Kenny Yu wanna a fuckin go, come! (*Runs off.*)

Ben   Kenny! I have never seen him lose it like that! He's gonna get killed.

Ade   Go help him then.

Ben   I ain't goin on my own, yu mad? Nuh, man.

Ade   Don't call me man.

Ben (*confused*)   Ade?

Ade   Yu think yu have the right to speak like us now?

Ben   Come on.

Ade   Is that how it goes now? Yu have the right? Yu stupid white bastard.

Ben   Don't . . .

Ade   Don't call yu that? (*Starts prodding him hard.*) Yu – are – a – stupid – white – bastard! I remember yu. Come on then. (*Shoves him.*) Come on.

Ben (*getting scared*)   Ade, man?

Ade   Yu deaf? Don't call me man.

Ben   We gotta help Kenny.

Ade   Yu help him. (*Exits.*)

Scene Five

Nathan'*s front door step. Same evening.*

Kenny *is standing by the door which is ajar.* **Nathan** *appears, he hands* **Kenny** *a glass of water.*

Kenny   Wass this?

Nathan   Water fer yer head. Yu'll thank me in the mornin.

Kenny   Come out for a drink I said.

Nathan   We were havin an early night.

Kenny   Yu fuckin lightweight.

Nathan   Oh Kenny, man, wat yu doin here, wat yu want?

Kenny   I missed yer.

Nathan (*embarrassed*)   Fuck off.

Kenny   It's true.

Nathan   Yer pissed.

Kenny   I know.

Nathan *hands him some photos.*

Kenny   Dis Zoe?

Nathan   All eight pounds of her.

Kenny   Fuck.

Nathan   Thass wat Melanie kept saying, all through the delivery.

Kenny   Yu saw it come out?

Nathan   Nuttin like it.

Kenny   Errgh, man.

Nathan   She was holdin on to my hand, nearly broke it off.

Kenny   Yu didn't feel sick or nuttin?

Nathan   How could I feel sick. It was my kid. So wat yu think of her?

Kenny   Yeah, man, she's nice.

Nathan   Nice!

Kenny   Awright she's beautiful.

Nathan   Thass better. Yu can keep that one.

Kenny   Nice one, Nate.

Nathan   Tell yer, man, no matter who yu are, how hard yu think yu are, when yu see that little baby for the first time yeah, and yu know it's yours, part of yu, yer gone.

Kenny   Good feeling?

Nathan   The best. I was born for this.

Kenny   She looks like Melanie.

Nathan   It's the cheeks, ennit? Yu don't think she's got my eyes? I think she's got my eyes.

Kenny   The poor cow's got enuff to worry about.

Nathan   Oi!

Kenny   Having yu fer a dad.

Nathan   Gimme back my picture.

Kenny   Move. Yu a dad, man. Shit, Nate!

Nathan   Ennit. I have to keep tellin myself, it don't feel true, hasn't quite sunk in, me a dad.

Kenny   Can't wait to see yu pushing a buggie about. Daddy Nathan.

Nathan   Yu won't be.

Kenny   Come again?

Nathan   We're moving to Manchester.

Kenny   When?

Nathan   As soon as we've found a house we like.

Kenny   We got houses in London, Nate.

Nathan   It's Melanie, she wants to move back closer to her mum.

Kenny   Wat do yu want?

Nathan   I got wat I want.

Kenny   Right little Midas.

Nathan   Wass that mean?

Kenny   Nuttin.

Nathan   Don't do a Ben on me.

Kenny   I ain't.

Nathan   I'm happy awright.

Kenny   Wat did I juss say?

Nathan   Yu are such a prick.

Kenny   Nate?

Nathan   Yu know this could be yu as well one day. I could be looking at pictures of yer kid. Stop getting led around by Ben all the time, yu muppet.

Kenny   He's gettin led round by me.

Nathan   The Palais!

Kenny   I like it deh.

Nathan   That bloke coulda killed yer tonight.

Kenny   He was lucky I didn't kill him. He was. Shoulda seen me, man, gave him a right caning.

Nathan   I'm gonna slap yu so hard in a minute.

Kenny   Rah, Nate turn bad man now.

Nathan   Talk to me.

Kenny   Bwoy, move. Yu love to chat.

Nathan   Wass goin on wid yu?

Kenny   Nuttin.

Nathan   Wat were yu thinking?

Kenny   I said it was nuttin.

Nathan   Don't gimme me that.

Kenny   Look, Ben started shoutin yeah . . .

Nathan   Ben!

Kenny   Let me finish, man.

Nathan   Yu'd jump in the Thames if Ben said.

Kenny   No.

Nathan   Are yu a sheep or wat?

Kenny   I said no.

Nathan   Still going to that dump.

Kenny   Fuck off.

Nathan   Yu fuck off. Yu wonder why I had to leave.

Kenny   I thought it was cos of Ben, know the truth now though. Yu wanted to get away from both of us.

Nathan   Yu were both doing my head in, I needed to go.

Kenny   And ware did yu go, Nate? Half a mile down the road, juss round the corner from me mum's? Twelve months I don't see yu, a whole year, not a phone call, man, nuttin.

Nathan   Yu would never have left Ben, yer too loyal.

Kenny   Is it my fault de bwoy love to hang round wid me?

Nathan   Will yu stop talkin like that. Will yu stop talkin shit. Why do yu love making an arsehole of yourself, every day of your life?

Kenny   Hey, I had enuff of yu dissing me, right.

Nathan   So go. Piss off. But don't bother coming back.

Kenny   I fuckin hate yu.

Nathan   Cos yu know I'm right. Yu pillock.

Kenny   Awright, man, ease up on the abuse.

Nathan   No. Grow up, yu stupid sap, Ben won't.

Ben (*enters*)   Ben won't wat? Kenny bwoy!

Kenny (*surprised*)   Ben?

Ben   Wat were yu doin runnin off like that?

Kenny   Wat are yu?

Ben   Lookin for yu. I was worried, man. That bloke gave yu a right beating. Yu awright?

Kenny   Yeah

Ben   That bloke didn't catch yer? Then again yu were runnin fast enuff.

Kenny   I'm fine.

Ben   Good. So, Ben won't wat?

Nathan   Grow up.

Ben   He still loves chattin behind people's back.

Nathan   I juss told yu didn't I? I'm going back to bed. (*To* **Kenny**.) Come round for dinner one night.

Ben (*laughs*)   Dinner?

Nathan   Any time.

Ben   Yu can't cook.

Nathan   How yu know?

Ben   I know.

Nathan   So I can't learn?

Ben   Must be Melanie. (*Swipes one of the photos.*) Who dis?

Kenny   Careful.

Ben   Who's the foetus?

Kenny   Ben!

Ben   She's tiny.

Nathan   She is my daughter.

Ben   Melanie finally dropped it then? Wass she doin wid red hair?

Nathan   She ain't got red hair.

Ben (*to* **Kenny**)   I bet the milkman's got red hair.

Nathan   Night, boys.

Ben   Night, Nathan.

Nathan   One of these days, Ben.

Ben   Yeah, wat?

Nathan   One of these fuckin days right.

Ben   Yeah wat!

Kenny   Guys, come on!

Nathan   Three hours on the train, thass all it is.

Ben   Fuckin snide.

Nathan   Wat did I do that was so wrong?

Ben (*teases*)   Ooooh!

Nathan   Juss tell me.

Ben   Kenny, give him a tissue, I think he's gonna cry.

Nathan   Such a wanker.

Ben   Excuse me?

Nathan   Yer not happy unless everyone is as sad as yu.

Ben   Yeah, come back here and say that to my face, Nathan.

Nathan   Talk to the door, Ben. (*Slams door behind him.*)

Ben   Come back and say that to my face. (*To* **Kenny**.) He's a snide right! Wat yu doin here?

Kenny   I jus wanted to see him. Wat were yu?

Ben (*cuts in*)   Three hours on the train, wass that?

Kenny   They're movin to Manchester.

Ben   Good.

Kenny   Yu don't mean that.

Ben   I don't care if I never see him again.

Kenny   Yer lying.

Ben   He's a fuckin snide.

Scene Six

The Palais.

Kenny *is facing* **Sandra**. *It is an uncomfortable silence.*

Sandra   So yu work in a bank then?

Kenny   Yep. Assistant manager.

Sandra   Oh yeah! I know who I'm comin to for a loan.

Kenny   How long yu known Sonya?

Sandra   'Bout three years. Yu don't look alike.

Kenny   Good. Wat yu do?

Sandra   Yu've asked me that.

Kenny   Sorry.

Sandra   Twice.

Kenny   Yu keepin score?

Sandra   Why yu so jumpy?

Kenny   I ain't.

Sandra   Like yu 'fraid of me, man. Never seen a black woman before?

Kenny   Don't be stupid.

Sandra   Ever bin out wid a black woman?

Kenny   Yeah.

Sandra   Wat about white women?

Kenny   Wat yu goin on wid?

Sandra   Do yu ever go for white women, Kenny?

Kenny   No.

Sandra   Not even once?

Kenny   No.

Sandra   Yer not lyin to me.

Kenny   I don't lie.

Sandra   Good, cos if yer one of dem fools, dem dogs who hang here chasin white skirt, yu can juss step.

Kenny   No worries.

Sandra   I don't know why yer sister chose to have her party here yu nuh. The state of these white girls, man, yu see 'em? Wid their high heels, tons of slap on their face.

Kenny   Yeah.

Sandra   Tell me summin, yer a man right. Right?

Kenny   Yeah.

Sandra   So wat is it about these fuckin girls that makes our men keep running to them? We got the same bits on our body as them. But the minute one of dem whores walks into a room yeah, all the men are runnin round like dogs, drooling over 'em. It makes me sick. Why do they do that?

Kenny   Can't help yer.

Sandra   Are white girls more sexy than we are? I don't think so. Do they scream more when guys do it to them? I can scream, I can scream loud.

Kenny   I dunno.

Sandra   Come on, Kenny, yu musta heard summin over the years, wat do black guys say, wat do they feel? Why do they do it?

Kenny   I don't know.

Sandra   Wass the matter wid yu?

Kenny   Nuttin. Maybe . . .

Sandra   Wat?

Kenny   Maybe they're scared of yer.

Sandra   Thass a lame excuse, I heard that shit before. Do I look scary to yu, am I scarin yu?

Kenny   No.

Sandra   So why yu look like yu wanna run fer yer life? Do all black women act the bloody same or summim? Yu know wat, fuck this. Fuck this! Don't blame us cos yu lot are fuckin insecure right? Maybe if yu lot treated us right in the first place, wid sum respect. I'm going for a white guy, yu spearchuckers are killin me. Fuckin black men, man, sorry-arsed niggers, yer brains are in yer dicks. A nice, fit, sincere, good-looking white guy yes! Time this gal felt appreciated.

Kenny   See yer then.

Sandra   Hold up, wait. Rum. Goes right to my head. Never let me near it.

Kenny   Don't drink it. We ain't all like him.

Sandra   Who?

Kenny   Yer boyfriend, ennit.

Sandra   Perceptive Kenneth. I like that. So wass yer story?

Kenny   Ain't got one. Oh don't do that. Why yu lot love to pull that face?

Sandra   Yu lot?

Kenny   Wid the attitude.

Sandra   Yu mean black women?

Kenny   I didn't say black. I meant women. All women.

Sandra   Maybe it's yu.

Kenny   It's yu women as well. Yu know how small yu make me feel? Like that.

Sandra   Don't be so soft. Yu ain't so bad. Yu can't like someone if yu don't like yerself.

Kenny   Wat yu tink yer smart now?

Sandra   Didn't get three A levels for nuttin.

Kenny   Yu get three A levels?

Sandra   Yes, Kenneth. Hear wat, I can read and write an all.

Kenny   So wat yu doin working in Argos wid yer three A levels?

Sandra   It's a job.

Kenny   Yu don't think yer wastin yerself?

Sandra   Yer sister works there.

Kenny   I rest my case.

Sandra   Yu got a nice smile.

Kenny *laughs*.

Sandra   Why yu so embarrassed by that?

Kenny   Do I look embarrassed?

Sandra   Yes. And I'm gonna bus yer head if yu keep doing that. Ain't no one told yu before got a nice smile? Cos yu have. To die for. Take the compliment.

Kenny   Awright I will.

Sandra   Startin now.

Kenny   Right now.

Sandra (*smiles*)   Good.

Kenny   Yu want go upstairs?

Sandra   Why?

Kenny   There's another dance floor, it plays better music.

Sandra   Thought yu didn't come here.

Kenny   I don't. I had a look when I came in.

Sandra   And then wat?

Kenny   Dance.

Sandra   We could dance down here.

Kenny   We could go somewhere else.

Sandra   And yu were doing so well.

Kenny   Look, yes or no, Sandra, yu dont have to run me down.

Sandra   Oh Kenny! Don't do a moody on me please. Ain't me thass coming out wid the dry chat. Do I look like I wanna be picked up? I didn't come here for that. I would never come here for that. All I wanna do is chat. If that ain't good enough for yu, then score wid one 'a dem white girls, there's plenty, go.

Kenny   It is. It is good enough for me.

Sandra   Yu sure?

Kenny   I'm sure.

Sandra   Yu positive?

Kenny   Yeah.

Sandra   Don't say yu are if yer not, Kenny.

Kenny   I am sure. Love to go on, ennit?

Sandra   Yeah. Now get me another drink.

Act Two

Scene One

A street.

Ben *is on his phone.*

Kenny   Hang up. I ain't messin about, hang up.

Ben   It's ringin.

Kenny   I ain't doin it.

Ben   Hello?

Kenny   I ain't doin it.

Ben   Is that (*Reads from the card.*) Cindy? Yeah I saw yer card, I was wondering where yu are. Full personal service, one hour. Is this a genuine photo? Yeah? Yeah! Awright yeah, can I have yer address? Wat? Why yu askin me that? Yu fuckin bitch. Yeah I hope yu get AIDS, yer slag. (*Hangs up suddenly.*)

Kenny   Wat?

Ben   Fuckin whore, man.

Kenny   Wat she say?

Ben   Don't worry about it.

Kenny   Tell me.

Ben   Don't get upset, Kenny, but she wanted to know if I was black. She says she don't do it wid black men. Don't worry about it, man, I still love yer.

Kenny   Who's worried? Yu think I care wat a whore thinks, it don't matter.

Ben   She must have a boyfriend who's black. He don't want another bro touchin her, ennit. She ain't worth the time, Kenny, she's a bitch.

Kenny   Can we go home please?

Ben   Hold up, let's not give up on the first go. (*Takes out some cards from his wallet.*) There must be one yu like.

Kenny   Jesus Christ, how many cards yu got?

Ben   Oh man, look at that one.

Kenny   Yu really think I wanna do this?

Ben   Yer sack is bursting, Kenny. I know how it feels.

Kenny   Yu done this before.

Ben   Couple of times.

Kenny   Why?

Ben   I get itches, man.

Kenny   Yer married.

Ben   Still get 'em. I don't fuck 'em, I juss get a blowjob an that. (*Eyes one.*) Lulu, French. Yeah man! (*Dials.*)

Kenny   Ben?

Ben   Back off. Yeah, French Beauty Lulu, yeah I see yer card, listen is that a genuine photo, she really looks like that?

Kenny (*grabs the phone*)   No.

Ben   Come on, she ain't no dog.

Kenny   No. (*Hangs up.*)

Ben   I'll go after yu.

Kenny   For fuck's sake!

Ben   Yu know wat, this is the lass time I ever do yu a favour.

Kenny   Yu call this a favour?

Ben   Juss get yer cock sucked.

Kenny   And yu wonder why Nate don't wanna see us.

Ben Nathan's a cunt. Marries sum bit, thinks he knows it all. Come on Kenny man, it's help me, help yu time. Look at her picture, look at her tits, don't tell me yu don't want 'em in yer face.

Kenny I don't.

Ben All I want to do is help yu catch up with Ade. He's had nuff pussy.

Kenny Hear wat, so have I.

Ben Wat, yu found yerself a woman now?

Kenny Yes.

Ben Lie.

Kenny I have.

Ben Yu ain't, Kenny.

Kenny Is that so strange?

Ben Name?

Kenny Sandra.

Ben Sandra? Is that the best yu can do?

Kenny It's her bloody name, awright?

Ben Come on.

Kenny I ain't making it up, Ben.

Ben Serious?

Kenny Yes.

Ben Well gimme sum details then. Ware yu meet her, who is she, how long?

Kenny She's a mate of my sister's, we met at the Palais a couple of nights ago.

Ben Nice one, bro. I bet she's white though, ennit, slapper!

Kenny She's black.

Ben Yu joke! (*Roars.*) Kenny boy, doing it wid him own kind at last. All the more reason to see this whore. Black women go like a train yeah? Yu don't get match fit, she'll run yu ragged.

Kenny I'm going home.

Ben Yer gettin yer cock sucked. And a fuck while yer at it.

Kenny I don't need to.

Ben Yu tellin me yu fucked it awready?

Kenny Yeah, I fucked it awready. She can't get enough of it. I got it, Ben. Hard to believe I know, but I finally got someone an it's real.

Ben Yu'll screw it up. Yu always do.

Kenny Watch yer mouth.

Ben Or wat! Wat do yu think yu can do to me, Kenneth? Wat did yu think yu could ever do to me? Yu think yer black, yu tink yer bad? Yu get a few pokes and yu tink yu the man? Yu want wake up. I know yu! I bet yu can't even do it properly. Juss behave yerself and do wat yer told right, or do yu want that girl laughin at yu every time yer givin her one?

Kenny I'm goin home.

Ben (*waves the card*)   Yu want it?

Kenny Denise is waiting for yer.

Ben 38DD. (*Dials.*)

Kenny Why did yu go to Nathan's that time?

Ben I was lookin for yu.

Kenny But yu hate his guts. Why did yu go?

Ben Still engaged

Kenny   Yu wanted to see him, cos yu were missin him, ennit? Cos this ain't yu, it ain't neither of us, why can't yu admit that? Go home, Ben.

Ben   I don't wanna go home. I don't want to see her face ever again.

Kenny   So she's got big teeth.

Ben   I didn't even fancy her. Yu know wat I did this morning, when I woke up? Started yawning and stretching right, 'member wat I said? Whacked her right in the face wid my elbow. Not one of her teeth come out. Not one! She still looks the same, Kenny. Wat they made of, iron?

Kenny   Yu hit yer wife.

Ben   I made out it was an accident, but she wouldn't stop cryin.

Kenny   Wass the matter wid yu? She's your wife. She is all yer ever gonna get.

Ben   I'll get loads, Kenny, I've had loads.

Kenny   Yu've had whores.

Ben   Go. Go and be laughed at by yer black woman. Amount of pussy I coulda had in my life, but nuh, had to hang round wid yu and only cos the black kids couldn't stand yu. Yu were a joke to them. Yu were lucky me and Nate took pity on yer, everyone was tellin us to drop yer.

Kenny   So drop me now. Do it. (**Kenny** *walks away*.)

Ben   She's laughin at yu, Ken, she's pissin herself.

Ben *presses his redial button again.*

Ben   Hello? Lulu ? Yeah I saw yer card. How much for an hour? Where are yer?

Scene Two

Palais nightclub.

Ade *is with* **Sandra**.

Ade   . . . So wass this guy's name?

Sandra   None of yer business.

Ade   I might know him.

Sandra   Yu don't.

Ade   How yu know?

Sandra   Go away.

Ade   Whoever he is, he muss be really special, if yer out in that dress. Yu aways look good in this dress. (*Squeezes her thigh.*)

Sandra   Get yer hand off me.

Ade   Easy, gal.

Sandra   I ain't yer gal.

Ade   Wat yu doin here, Sandra?

Sandra   Havin a drink.

Ade   Yu wouldn't be seen dead comin here. It's cos of me, ennit?

Sandra   Yu wish.

Ade   So wass this guy like?

Sandra   Yer white slag's wavin to yer.

Ade   'Im givin it to yu good?

Sandra   Dirty bastard.

Ade   Does he stroke the back of yer neck like I used to?

Sandra   He's juss a friend.

Ade   Friend!

Sandra   Go away, please.

Ade   Nuh, man, I'm stayin right here till 'yer friend' comes back.

Sandra   Yu know wat, it muss be sad bin yu, Ade. Havin to prove to yerself, every night, that yer fit, yer all man. Yer come a long way from the shy guy who didn't know ware to put it.

Ade   Hey, I aways knew ware to put it.

Sandra   And when yu finally did, it kept on comin out, 'member? 'Is it in Sandra? Sandra is it in?'

Ade   Yer chattin shit. Bitch.

Sandra   Don't feel too bad, yu were awright, after a while. I bet thass why yu go fer yer white girls, ennit, cos they tink yer givin them the fuck of the century wid yer third leg. See yer one over there, I bet yu only have to touch her and she's creamin her knickers, ennit? But I know the trut, so do a lot of sistas who know niggers like yu.

Ade   Yer frigid.

Sandra   Old.

Ade   Can't handle wass on offer.

Sandra   I've seen bigger ones than yours. Big!

Ade   And yu girls have the nerve to wonder why we go lookin elsewhere.

Sandra   Cos yer sad?

Ade   All yu lot come wid is this attitude, 'is who yu look pon', all that shit. Especially yu, yu love to put that on, yu call that sexy? Every time yu and that bitch Yvonne get together.

Sandra   Don't call my friend a bitch.

Ade Yu know it ain't yu.

Sandra Yer the bitch.

Ade When we first went out, yu had summim.

Sandra Mug, written on my forehead.

Ade Yer mates had nuttin but big mouths on them, but yu were different from them, I saw it the minute I laid eyes on yer.

Sandra Juss hurry up and come fer the rest of yer things right.

Ade Yer better than them and yu know it.

Sandra I am one a' dem! Go back to yer white whore.

Ade So yu find yerself another African prince then. Wat makes yu think he's gonna be any different than me?

Sandra He ain't African.

Ade Yes he is

Sandra No he ain't.

Ade Don't lie, Sandra.

Sandra I ain't lyin.

Ade I know yu, yu can't help yerself. Yu love yer darkie men too much. I know. Juss like I know that white bitch over there wants me to fuck her tonight.

Sandra Do yu want to go to jail?

Ade Yu jealous?

Sandra Look at her. She don't look much older than yer sister, man. Stay or go, cos I don't care.

Ade Yu do.

Ade *touches her thigh again.* **Sandra** *doesn't push him away until* **Kenny** *enters, carrying drinks.*

Sandra   Kenny. Ware yu bin?

Kenny   Bloody queue was a mile long. Awright, Ade? (*Sits next to* **Sandra**.)

Ade   Him? Yu tellin me it's him?

Sandra   Yu know each other?

Ade   No, no, no, man.

Sandra   No wat?

Ade   I'm not havin it.

Sandra   Yer not havin it?

Ade   Yu and him.

Sandra   It's none of yer business.

Ade   Fuck's sake, gal, him? He ain't nuttin.

Sandra   He ain't yu.

Ade   Awright, Sandra, enuff's enuff yeah wat yu want?

Sandra   I want yu to go.

Ade   Me dump the bitch, fine she's dumped. (*Waves.*) Laters. I don't care about her.

Sandra   Nor do I, fuck whoever yu like.

Ade   But thass all she is, juss a fuck. I don't care about her. I don't care about none of them. Ain't it yu I aways come back to though?

Sandra   Well I'm tired of it yeah. Sick an tired. The way yu make me feel, about myself.

Ade   Well he ain't no better. I fuck 'em cos I can, Sandra. He can't even do that. He's desperate. No white gal will touch him. Look at him, look at him juss fuckin standin there like sum fool.

Sandra   Leave him alone.

Ade   Yu comin?

Sandra   Leave me alone.

Kenny   Come on, Ade.

Ade   YU SHUT YER MOUT! DON'T TOUCH ME!

Sandra   Ade!

Ade   I'm better than yu.

Sandra   Juss go.

Ade   I'm better than yu.

Sandra   Now.

Ade *leaves*.

Sandra   Wass that about?

Kenny   We were at school together

Sandra   And?

Kenny   And nuttin, guy's mad.

Sandra   Wat did he mean white girls wouldn't touch yu? Yer one of dem. I shoulda guessed. Yu come here all the time, ennit?

Kenny   No.

Sandra   Kenny, don't lie.

Kenny   Awright yeah, but I don't do that no more, I swear.

Sandra   Look it's OK. It's none of my business.

Kenny   Yu wanted to come here again, I didn't.

Sandra   If thass wat yu want, gwan. Don't let me stop yer.

Kenny   It's not wat I want. I lied cos I wanted to see yu again.

Sandra   Kenny?

Kenny I know, yu've told me, yu juss want us to be friends, yu ain't ready for nuttin else.

Kenny *watches* **Sandra** *who in turn is watching* **Ade***.*

Kenny Well I know why yu wanted to come here again.

Sandra Wat yu take me for?

Kenny Who's lyin now? Wat did yu see in him?

Sandra Same thing she does.

Kenny She ain't all that. Yer fitter than that.

Sandra Trying to make me feel better, Kenneth?

Kenny Yeah.

Sandra *leans forward and kisses him on the cheek.* **Kenny** *takes this as read and kisses her back.*

Kenny Was that awright?

Sandra *laughs.*

Kenny Wat yu laughin for?

Sandra It was nice. Yu shouldn't say things like that. Don't look so worried.

Kenny It's awright, I'm cool.

Sandra Good.

Kenny Look when I asked yu was it awright, I didn't mean that I was, that I was, yu know soft cos I ain't right, I ain't like, I juss thought yu wanted me to kiss yu, but I'm sorry if yu didn't.

Sandra Kenny.

Kenny SHIT!

Sandra Will yu please calm down. It's awright. Wat am I going to do wid yu huh?

Sandra *glances over at* **Ade** *again, getting off with his girl. She kisses* **Kenny** *on the lips.*

Sandra   Finish yer drink.

Kenny   Why were we?

Sandra   Come on.

Scene Three

Nathan's *front door step.*

Nathan *opens a Mothercare shopping bag and looks inside.*

Nathan   How much was all this?

Kenny   Don't worry about it, there was a sale.

Nathan   I'm juss trying to picture it. Yu in Mothercare. We got baby clothes coming out of our ears.

Kenny   Now yu got sum more. Yu gonna invite me in or wat?

Nathan   Yeah in a minute, juss let me have this. Melanie don't like me smoking in the house wat wid the baby and that.

Kenny   She's really beautiful.

Nathan   I know. And yer final answer is?

Kenny   I dunno.

Nathan   The christening's in two weeks.

Kenny   Wat yu want a godfather for? Yu don't even go to church.

Nathan   Melanie's mum. She's into all that. I juss do wat I'm told, mate.

Nathan   Makes for a quiet life. Well?

Kenny   I dunno.

Nathan   Wass there to know?

Kenny   It'll feel funny, wat wid Ben.

Nathan   We have to chat about him?

Kenny   Well I don't need to ask ware yu stand on it.

Nathan   Ennit.

Kenny   If he was here now, yu'd be askin him.

Nathan   No.

Kenny   He's still yer best mate.

Nathan   Yes or no, Kenny?

Kenny   I'll think about it.

Nathan   Don't strain yerself.

Kenny   I'm really worried about him. He's never done anything like this before.

Nathan   Why? He brought it on himself.

Kenny   We talkin about the same Ben here?

Nathan   The same Ben who wouldn't come to my wedding, the same Ben who blew me out on his.

Kenny   He ain't no wife beater.

Nathan   He hit her.

Kenny   Well we can't all be like yu. Wid yer nice house, wife, kid.

Nathan   This is Ben talking. I can hear his voice.

Kenny   Yu know he only married her to get back at yu.

Nathan   Wass there to get back at? I fell in love for fuck's sake. This is all so stupid. Can we change the subject please, if yer not going to be Zoe's godfather, least yu can do is stay for dinner? Give Sandra a bell. I want to meet her.

Kenny   She's busy.

Nathan   Wid wat?

Kenny   Work.

Nathan   We'll have to make it next week then. I'll tell
Mel. How about Thursday?

Kenny   Watever.

Nathan   Don't sound too eager.

Kenny   Will yu shut up about dinner please, yu sound like
a nob.

Nathan   Touchy.

Kenny   Yu love to go on.

Nathan   Awright.

Kenny   Asking me to be godfather. Cos I got a girlfriend
now, I'm respectable now.

Nathan   Up to yu.

Kenny   Then wat? We go out on double dates, meal,
cinema, be best man at my wedding. We have homes in the
country, women at our side, kids at our feet.

Nathan   Don't be a prick all yer life.

Kenny   Couldn't yu have juss fucked Melanie?

Nathan   Say wat yu feel, Ken.

Kenny   Yu shoulda juss fucked her.

Nathan   Yeah I shoulda juss fucked her, like a fucking lad
I shoulda fucked her. But there is juss one problem, Kenny,
I'm not a lad. I never was. Yeah I had a laugh, I got pissed,
but all I was doing was waiting, waiting for someone special
to come into my life. Yu got someone special in yer life now,
right? Haven't yer?

Kenny   How do I keep her happy, Nate ? How do I do it?

Nathan   Be yerself.

Kenny   Yu always say that, yer always tellin me that, be yerself!

Nathan   And yu never listen.

Kenny   I don't know wat we have.

Nathan   She's yer girlfriend, yu fool.

Kenny   She ain't my girlfriend. We met a couple of weeks ago at my sister's party. We went out lass night, she took me back to hers. Yu know wat I'm saying, yu know were I'm going wid this?

Nathan   Yeah I think so.

Kenny   It was crap. I was crap. I didn't know wat I was doing, not a clue. She knew it too. So nice about it though, made it easy for me, she's always doin that. If thass been myself.

Nathan   Did it ever occur to yu in that stupid head of yours, yu weren't bin yerself, yu spent half yer life thinking about it, how yer gonna do it, but when it comes down to it, yu ain't got a clue.

Kenny   I'm twenty-nine, I should be fuckin her brains out, make her scream her head off.

Nathan   Listen, when I first saw Melanie man, I tell yer, I knew she was the one for me. But that didn't stop me making a prat of myself in front of her. Yu think I knew what we were doing when we first did it? I was well nervous, shaking like fuck. She had to calm me down. But afterwards it didn't matter, cos we were so right for each other.

Kenny   Oh enuff wid that corny shit, Nate.

Nathan   It's true. Laugh all yu want, Kenny, but it's true. For me anyway.

Kenny   But yu said yu were waiting for someone. So yu didn't care who it was. Yu were desperate to be loved. So how different are yu from Ben?

Nathan   I love my wife.

Kenny   Yu only went with her cos she got pregnant, Ben said.

Nathan   Ben's a liar.

Kenny   Yu only knew her five minutes.

Nathan   So wat, who cares how long yu knew her, who cares about anything at all when yer sure about yer feelins? I love Melanie. She's everything to me. I think about her all the time, I hate it when we're apart, we cuddle up to each other in bed all mornin, every Sunday, read the papers. All that corny shit, Kenny, and I love it.

Kenny   Yer the lucky one then.

Nathan   It can still happen to yu.

Kenny   So wat I can't come in now?

Nathan   Up to yu.

Kenny   She's me god-daughter.

Scene Four

Sandra*'s flat.*

Sandra *watches as* **Ade** *comes into the living room carrying his bag.*

Ade   Right, got the rest of my things, I'm gone yeah.

Sandra   So which one of dem slags yu movin in wid then?

Ade   I thought yu didn't wanna talk to me?

Sandra   I don't.

Ade   So why yu chattin?

Sandra   I need an address. To forward yer mail.

Ade   Yu couldn't juss ask me that?

Sandra   Don't read anything into that.

Ade   Am I?

Sandra   I know yer looks.

Ade   I'm still at me mum's. Awright?

Sandra   Thank yu. Goodbye.

Ade (*takes a video from his bag*)   Sure yu don't want this one?

Sandra   Why?

Ade   It's good.

Sandra   It's French.

Ade   Yes or no?

Sandra   No. Yu better not have messed up my Buffy collection.

Ade   Heaven forbid. I suppose yu'll be movin him in now.

Sandra   No.

Ade   Yu love him?

Sandra   I told yu.

Ade   He's juss a friend, yeah watever. Can't believe I let this happen, yu nuh.

Sandra   Yu let this happen?

Ade   Runnin to him.

Sandra   Lass time I checked, Ade, I had a mind of my own.

Ade (*takes out another video*)   Wat about this?

Sandra   No.

Ade   It won four Oscars.

Sandra   I don't want yer videos. I don't want nuttin of yours in my flat.

Ade   Did he tell yu what him and his mates did to me at school?

Sandra   Yeah.

Ade   And?

Sandra   Ain't my fault yu couldn't stick up for yerself.

Ade   Yu sound like the teachers.

Sandra   Was it that bad?

Ade   Yeah it was.

Sandra   Don't take it out on me.

Ade   Wat do yu expect when I find yer goin wid him, why him, Sandra!

Sandra   I'm talking about the past two years.

Ade   Twice, I fucked around twice.

Sandra   Three times, don't lie. And those are the ones I know about.

Ade   Well blame him then.

Sandra   Yu ain't got a mind of yer own?

Ade   Every mornin when I had to go into that school, I was shakin wid fear. Till I was fifteen. Every single day his precious white friends takin turns beating me up. I didn't know who I hated more, him or dem.

Sandra   So yu wanna hurt them now?

Ade   Yeah.

Sandra   And yu wanna fuck deh women, no matter who yu hurt along the way.

Ade   I didn't mean to.

Sandra   But yu did. Yu don't do that. Yu don't take me wid yu. Wat I am, wat we had, should be enough for yu.

Ade   I'm sorry.

Sandra   Fuck sorry. I had it wid sorry. Yu know wat, I don't think yu hate 'em cos they beat yu up. I think yu hate 'em cos they chose Kenny and not yu.

Ade   Wat?

Sandra   All dem white boys. Kenny standin wid dem.

Ade   Were yu there?

Sandra   Yu wanted to be standin wid dem.

Ade   Yu weren't bloody there.

Sandra   Tell me I'm wrong.

Ade   Laters.

Sandra   Ade?

Ade   Fuck off.

Sandra   Look me in the eye.

Ade   Yer talkin shit.

Sandra   Look me in the eye. Tell me yu weren't lyin on the ground yeah, getting kicked around, thinking to yerself, 'Choose me, choose me, I'm better than he is, choose me!'

Ade   No.

Sandra   True, ennit?

Ade   No.

Sandra   Ade? It's true.

Ade   Fuck off.

Sandra   Knew it.

Ade   Yu don't know nuttin.

Sandra   I know. Yu were juss too dark.

Ade   Yu fuckin cow. Yu think I wanna be white?

Sandra   Don't yu? Tell the truth, Ade. Juss once tell me the truth please.

Ade   No.

Sandra   Yer lying.

Ade   I don't want to be white.

Sandra   Yes yu do.

Ade   Sandra!

Sandra   And yu want the same for me. Ennit? Ennit? Ain't that the answer, Ade?

Ade   The answer's no.

Sandra   So why yu always telling me I'm better than my friend?

Ade   Cos yu are.

Sandra   Confusing the fuck outta me. The worst thing is, I know yer right. I spoke to Yvonne, New Year's Eve?

Ade   She tell yu?

Sandra   It's wat she didn't say. Look on her face when I brought it up. Tek that fuckin smile off yer face.

Ade   I weren't smilin.

Sandra   I feel it every day, is that wat yu wanna hear? Hearin her and them go on about shit, runnin men down, mek up noise wherever they are. I feel like killin them sometimes. When I'm wid dem, people don't see me, they see black.

Ade   Feisty nigger woman wid attitude.

Sandra   I don't like it when I think like that. And I ain't ready to step out, Ade, especially to be with you. Yu want everything from me but yu give back nuttin.

Ade   Yu think yer gonna get that from him?

Kenny   He will suck the life out of yu. I ain't gonna stand round and let that happen.

Sandra   Yu don't have a say in wat happens to me.

Ade   Yu can't tell me all that about yer friends and expect me to walk. Not when there's a chance.

Sandra   Why are yu doin this to me?

Ade   I don't want yu seein him.

Sandra   Why yu love doing this to me?

Ade   Yu know he can't make yu feel better than I can.

Sandra   Yer as screwed up as he is.

Ade   Don't compare me to him.

Sandra   Why not? Why can't I do that, wat yu afraid of?

Ade   I'm done with white women.

Sandra   I don't want to hear yu, I don't want to see yu.

Ade   I don't need them.

Sandra   Do I look like I care?

Ade   I got yu, all I wanted was yu, the real yu. We stay in and watch telly all day like we used to yeah? When we first went out. I go out for KFC. Then we stay in bed all evening and watch *Blind Date*. Sandra?

Sandra   No.

Ade   Come on.

Sandra   I ain't letting yu confuse me.

Ade   I'm not.

Sandra   Yu are, Ade. Yu bloody are.

Scene Five

Sandra's *flat.* **Kenny** *is typing away on his laptop.*

Kenny   How much do yu think yu can save each month?

Sandra   Dunno. Forty?

Kenny   That all?

Sandra   Wat?

Kenny   Yu won't see much of a pension wid that?

Sandra   It's all I can afford.

Kenny   How much yu earn a week?

Sandra   A hundred and ninety.

Kenny   That all?

Sandra   Yes!

Kenny   Ain't much.

Sandra   It'll do me.

Kenny   Yu got this place.

Sandra   Housing Association.

Kenny   But it's nice.

Sandra   Oi! Do yu know how much rent I'd be paying if sum landlord had his hands on it? Yu know ware I'd be? Back at me mum's.

Kenny   Yu should speak to someone from yer own bank. Ask to speak to yer financial consultant.

Sandra   All I want is advice.

Kenny   Not my special field though.

Sandra   Yer a bloody bank manager.

Kenny   Assistant. Awright, yu want to see a decent pension, start putting a few coins in.

Sandra   So how much then?

Kenny   'Bout a hundred? Hey, don't knock it, keep saving, and yu could have a hundred thousand by the time yer sixty. Juss buy a few less CDs a month.

Sandra   Shut up.

Kenny   Or video.

Kenny *kisses* **Sandra**. **Sandra** *pretends to enjoy it.*

Sandra   More wine? (*Goes in the kitchen.*) Look, I don't know if I can afford a hundred.

Kenny   Yu can, see yer . . .

Sandra   Financial consultant, I heard.

Kenny   Have I done summin?

Sandra   Wat?

Kenny   Yer in a mood.

Sandra   And it has to be about yu.

Kenny   Sorry.

Sandra   Stop apologising. Bad day at work.

Kenny   Wanna talk?

Sandra   No. Put that away.

Kenny   Yu wanted my advice.

Sandra   Yu've advised.

Kenny   Look why don't we get married!

Sandra (*stunned*)   Excuse me?

Kenny   Married.

Sandra   Oh man.

Kenny   Yer the one.

Sandra   Kenny?

Kenny Don't we?

Sandra We need to talk.

Kenny No, don't say that.

Sandra Yu expect me to say yes right now?

Kenny Yu think I bin sudden.

Sandra Wat yu on, man?

Kenny Well so wat? Who cares about bin sudden, who cares about anythin when yer sure about yer feelins? I am. At least think about it yeah, don't come out wid we gotta talk.

Sandra Yu don't love me, Kenny, yu juss love the idea.

Kenny Yu fucked him.

Sandra I'm sorry?

Kenny All his videos have gone.

Sandra He came round today to get his stuff.

Kenny Then yu fucked him and yer going back to him.

Sandra Kenny . . .

Kenny Guys like him, man, all my life.

Sandra Listen to me.

Kenny Don't yu think I wanna be like him, like all of them?

Sandra I did not fuck him. I wanted to. I thought about it. But I didn't do it.

Kenny Oh man. Come here. Come here.

Sandra Kenny.

Kenny (*kisses her*) I really thought that was it yu nuh, total blow out, game over, same old shit.

Sandra Kenny wait, juss wait man. I ain't gonna marry yu.

Kenny   But the other night though.

Sandra   Wass sex. Fer fuck's sake.

Kenny   Awright, we'll carry on as before then.

Sandra   No.

Kenny   Why?

Sandra   Yu know why. Jeez, yu men are doing my head in. I can't carry yu.

Kenny   That wat it feels like?

Sandra   Yes.

Kenny   It never happens, it never happens to me. I'm aways missin out, me. Yu know why, cos, cos, I can't get a handle on it yu know. Never know wat to do. I see a girl right, look at her and that, she looks back, yer heart's goin mad, tellin yu thass it, go fer it, but yer head, fuckin head right, fuckin head sayin na, na, don't be silly, yer wrong, man! So yu give it up, yer let it go. But wat if it was right, that was it, she was the one, wat if I juss said summin, stop believin that yer crap, yer nuttin, and believed, juss believed she liked yer. I don't have to think, I don't have to do nuttin, or prove myself, fuck wat colour yu are, fuck how yu think yu look, juss feel it, let yerself feel it.

Kenny *packs away his laptop. He takes* **Sandra**'s *hand and kisses it before leaving.*

Scene Six

Palais Nightclub.

Ben *is with* **Kenny**.

Kenny   I wasn't sweatin. My heart weren't pumpin. Or shakin like a leaf. None of that. Not a trace of wat went on before. Nerves of steel. I juss did it.

Ben   Was she white?

Kenny   Yes.

Ben   Whore. Find yerself a black woman, wass the matter wid yer?

Kenny   I did remember.

Ben   Stealin our women!

Kenny   Kiss my shiny black arse awright.

Ben   So yu asked this whore out then?

Kenny   Yes.

Ben   So wat she say?

Kenny   She went all embarrassed, face was turnin red, man, I was thinkin, oh fuck, blow out, feel like a right turd.

Ben   Nuttin unusual about that.

Kenny   I was thinkin again, when am I ever gonna get it right?

Ben   She said no.

Kenny   No.

Ben   She said yes?!

Kenny   Yes.

Ben   She said yes to yu?

Kenny   Yes.

Ben   Gwan.

Kenny   Thank yu.

Ben   Gwan!

Kenny   She gave me her number.

Ben   Yu call her?

Kenny   Yeah.

Ben   Details!

Kenny   I called her.

Ben   And?

Kenny   Left a message on her machine.

Ben   She called yu back, and?

Kenny   She didn't.

Ben   Wat?

Kenny   Called me back.

Ben   Wat yu mean she didn't call yu back?

Kenny   She didn't call me back.

Ben   Yu asked for her number, she gave it yer.

Kenny   No, I didn't ask for her number, she juss gave it to me.

Ben   So why ain't she called yu back?

Kenny   Ask her.

Ben   Fuckin whore.

Kenny   Rang her back twice.

Ben   Wass she say?

Kenny   Nuttin, spoke to the machine.

Ben   Fuckin whore.

Kenny   Oh well.

Ben   Wat yu mean 'oh well'? This is bad, man.

Kenny   I know it is.

Ben   So wat yu smilin for?

Kenny   Yu want me go goin back bin miserable? I weren't nervous. I saw her, liked her, asked her out. Thinkin didn't come into it. I juss did it.

Ben   She blew yu out, yu fool.

Kenny   Her loss.

Ben   Denzil!

Kenny   I ain't bodered no more.

Ben   Wat brought this on?

Kenny   Nuttin.

Ben   It was that Sandra slag.

Kenny   Don't call her that.

Ben   Slag, man.

Kenny   Ben! Wat the fuck.

Ben   Wass that mean?

Kenny   It means wat it means, wat the fuck.

Ben   Juss hurry up and find a woman, man.

Kenny   Yes, Dad.

Ben   A black woman, leave our ones alone.

Kenny   I heard yu rang Nathan.

Ben   Yeah, I thought I might as well, yu know. He's suffered enough.

Kenny   Wat did yu say?

Ben   Don't be a stranger, keep in touch.

Kenny   Nice one.

Ben   He really loves her, ennit?

Kenny   Yeah.

Ben   Denise's kicked me out.

Kenny   Yeah?

Ben   Her dad wants me dead.

Kenny   Wat about yer job?

Ben   Fuck yer job. His words.

Kenny (*sees his friend crying*)   Ben?

Ben (*wipes his face*)   Juss find yerself a nice girl, Kenny, awright.

Kenny   Awright.

Ben   Yu deserve one.

Kenny   Thanks.

Blackout.